Electrici

Many Shocking Jokes For Electricians

Published by Glowworm Press
7 Nuffield Way
Abingdon OX14 1RL
By Chester Croker

Jokes For Electricians

These jokes will shock you. These jokes for electricians are so shocking they will put a spark back in your life.

Some of them are old, but some of them are current, and while we don't want to plug them too much, we hope you enjoy these bright gags - our collection of the very best electrician jokes and puns. You're bound to laugh at them until it Hertz.

FOREWORD

When I was asked to write a foreword to this book I was very flattered.

That is until I was told by the author, Chester Croker, that I was the complete last resort and that everyone else he had approached had said they couldn't or wouldn't' do it!

I have known Chester for a number of years and his ability to create funny jokes is amazing. He is quick-witted and an expert at crafting clever puns and amusing gags and I feel he is the ideal man to put together a joke book about our profession.

He is like us in that he can think on his feet very quickly, and I know he will be glad you have bought this book, as he has an expensive lifestyle to maintain.

Electric Ian

Table of Contents

Chapter 1: Electrician Jokes

If you're looking for electrician jokes and funny electrical jokes you've come to the right place.

Electrician jokes are always current! And it takes a real bright spark to come up with these electrical jokes and puns. Your brain definitely has to be wired in a certain type of way to conductor a conversation using these jokes.

Some of these jokes are old, but some of them are current, and while we don't want to plug them too much, we hope you enjoy our collection of the very best electrician jokes and puns. You're bound to laugh at them until it Hertz.

We've got some great one-liners to start with, plenty of quick fire questions and answers themed gags, some story led jokes and as a bonus some cheesy pick-up lines for electricians. This mixture of jokes is guaranteed to get you laughing.

Chapter 2: One Liner Electrician Jokes

I finally managed to get rid of that nasty electrical charge I've been carrying. I'm ex-static!

The electrician who got arrested for eating batteries is to be charged in the morning.

My friend told me how electricity is measured and I was like, Watt?

I went to an AC/DC concert last night. It was shocking.

Old electricians never die. They just lose contact.

Lee, the electrician, accidentally blew the power to an ice making factory.

It has now gone into liquidation.

I was at work today and my boss told me to lighten up. Fair enough, I suppose; as I am an electrician on a film set.

I was sacked from my job as an electrician at the prison service for refusing to repair an electric chair. I told them it was a death trap.

Cheeky sign seen on the side of an electrician's van – "Let Us Get Rid of Your Shorts."

My last girlfriend left me for an electrician. He promised her the earth.

Is a successful politician a power transformer?

I have a long list of electricians who happen to be good jokers. Sadly, your name has been OHM -mitted.

My friend, who has mild epilepsy, is an electrician.

He's a light fitter.

Two atoms were walking down the street one day, when one of them exclaimed, "Oh no - I've lost an electron!" "Are you sure?" the other one asked. "Yes," replied the first one, "I'm positive."

I have always wanted to have a power plant. Yesterday, I planted a light bulb.

An electrician wanted to buy something for his dreadful boss, so he bought him a new chair. His boss won't let him plug it in though.

Sign seen on the side of an electrician's van: - "Power to the people."

Never trust an electrician with no eyebrows.

I had a dream about a dyslexic electrician last night.

It was well wired.

Old electricians never die; they just do it until it Hertz.

Did you hear about the trainee electrician who stole a calendar?

He got twelve months.

I got called pretty yesterday and it felt good. Actually, the full sentence was "You're a pretty bad electrician." but I'm choosing to focus on the positive.

Did you hear about the miracle of the blind electrician?

He picked up a hammer and saw.

Colin the electrician arrives home at 2am.

His wife asks him "Wire you insulate?" to which he replies,

"Watt's it to you? I'm Ohm, aren't I?"

An electrician friend of mine said I should put something away for a rainy day. I've gone for an umbrella.

People are usually shocked when they find out I'm not a very good electrician.

Yesterday, an electrician's wife asked him to pass her lipstick but he passed her a super-glue stick instead by mistake. She still isn't talking to him.

A daft electrician friend of mine has just started tap dancing lessons. He's not very good though – he keeps falling in the sink!

If you plant a light bulb in your garden, does it grow into a power plant?

I used to go out with a female electrician.

Unfortunately, she was shocking in bed.

Chapter 3: Question and Answer Electrician Jokes

Q: What kind of van does an electrician drive?

A: *A Volts-wagon.*

Q: Why do fluorescent lights hum?

A: *Because they can't remember the words.*

Q: How do you pick out a dead battery from a pile of good ones?

A: *It's got no spark.*

Q: What did the light bulb say to the generator?

A: *I really get a charge out of you.*

Q: Why are electricians always up to date?

A: *Because they are "Current specialists."*

Q: What is the definition of a shock absorber?

A: *A careless electrician!*

Q: What would you call a power failure?

A: *A current event.*

Q: Why did the lights go out?

A: *Because they liked each other.*

Q: What did Godzilla say when he ate the nuclear power plant?

A: *"Shocking!"*

Q: How many electricians does it take to change a light bulb?

A: *Just one, but then he will re-wire it to bring it up to building regulations code.*

Q: What is an electrician's favourite mobile messaging app?

A: *WattsApp!*

Q: What's grey, crispy and hangs from the ceiling?

A: *An amateur electrician.*

Q: What's the difference between an ugly woman and a battery?

A: *A battery has a positive side.*

Q: Why did Mr. Ohm marry Mrs. Ohm?

A: *Because he couldn't resistor.*

Q: What do you call a bad electrician?

A: *A shock absorber.*

Q: What is an electrician's favourite ice cream flavour?

A: *Shock-o-lot.*

Q: What do you call a Russian electrician?

A: *Switchitonanov.*

Q: What do you call a carpenter working in an electrical panel?

A: *Dead.*

Q: How do you know when a union electrician is dead?

A: *The doughnut rolls out of his hand.*

Q: What does an electrician say to another electrician when they meet up?

A: *Watts up?*

Q: What is an electrician's favourite Tom Jones song?

A: *Wire, wire, wire Delilah.*

Q: Who is an electrician's favourite superhero?

A: *Resis-Thor!*

Q: What do electricians call their apprentice?

A: *Shock Absorber!*

Q: Which is the smallest city?

A: *Electri-city.*

Q: Did you hear about the stupid gardener?

A: *He planted a light bulb and thought he would get a power plant.*

Q: What do you call worms that chew up electric wires?

A: *Electro-maggots.*

Q: Why are electricians always up to date?

A: *Because they are "current specialists".*

Q: Why was the free electron so sad?

A: *It had nothing to be positive about.*

Q: What do electricians chant when they meditate?

A: *Ohm.*

Q: What would a barefooted man get if he stepped on an electric fence?

A: *A pair of shocks.*

Q: Where do electricians get their supplies?

A: *Ohm Depot.*

Q: What do you call a detective electrician?

A: *Sherlock Ohms.*

Q: What is an electrician's most hated workwear?

A: *Shorts Circuit.*

Q: What did Thomas Edison's mother say to her son?

A: *Of course I'm proud you invented the electric light bulb. Now turn it off and get to sleep.*

Q: What did the electrician name his dog?

A: *Sparky.*

Q: What do all electricians have in common?

A: *They all have their faults.*

Q: Why was the free electron sad?

A: *It had nothing to be positive about.*

Q: What did the journeyman electrician say when asked to name two transformers?

A: *Decepticons and Autobots.*

Q: What do electricians call a power outage?

A: *A current event.*

Q: What did the light bulb say to the generator?

A: *"I really get a charge out of you!"*

Q: What's the temperament of most electricians?

A: *They're down to earth.*

Q: What did the baby light bulb say to mummy light bulb?

A: *"I love you watts and watts."*

Q: Why did the lights go out?

A: *Because they liked each other.*

Q: What's the difference between a woman and a battery?

A: *A battery has a positive side.*

Q: What did the light bulb say to the electric generator?

A: *You spark up my life.*

Q: What is the definition of a shock absorber?

A: *A careless electrician.*

Q: Why do transformers hum?

A: *Because they don't know the words!*

Q: How does an electrician tell if he's working with AC or DC power?

A: *If it's AC, his teeth chatter when he grabs the conductors. If it's DC, they just clamp together.*

Q: What did the light bulb say to the generator?

A: *I really get a charge out of you.*

Q: Why did the cannibal electrician get disciplined by his boss?

A: *For buttering up his clients.*

Q: How do you pick out a dead battery from a pile of good ones?

A: *It's got no spark!*

Q: What do you call an electrician who is happy every Monday?

A: *Retired.*

Chapter 4: Short Electrician Jokes

An electrician called Colin and a roofer called Gary were working on a building site.

Gary is up on the roof and accidentally cuts off his ear, and he yelled down to Colin "Hey - look out for my ear I just cut off."

Colin looks around and calls up to Gary, "Is this your ear?"

Gary looks down and says, "Nah! Mine had a pencil behind it!"

My tight-fisted brother-in-law doesn't want to pay for an electrician to re-wire his house so he's going to try and do it himself.

"How hard can it be?" he said.

I think he's in for a shock.

A superconductor walks into a bar.

The bartender says, "Get out. We don't serve your kind here."

The superconductor left without resistance.

My wife told me the spark between us had gone.

So I tasered her.

I'll ask her again when she wakes up.

Counsellor: "So what have you learned from your husband's death?"

Wife: "Brown is live and brown is neutral."

Two electricians are having a conversation about sex. The first electrician says that sex is 75% work and 25% pleasure. The second electrician says that sex is 25% work and 75% pleasure.

Getting nowhere, they decide to ask their apprentice's opinion.

"Sex is all pleasure," says the apprentice.

"Why do you say that?" reply the electricians.

To which the apprentice replies, "Because if it there is any work involved, you two have me do it."

An electrician in my area went to jail for dealing drugs.

I've been one of his customers for over five years and I had no clue he was an electrician.

A man with a hearing problem joined a power plant for a tour.

The guide told the group that they wouldn't start the tour until they answered his question: "What is the unit of power equal to one joule per second called?"

The man with the hearing problem hadn't heard the question, so he raised his hand and asked, "What?" (*What = Watt*)

An electrician took his cross-eyed spaniel to the vet.

The vet picked the dog up, gave him a thorough examination and then said, "Sorry, I'm going to have to put him down."

The electrician said, "Oh no! It's not that bad is it?"

The vet replied, "No, he's just very heavy."

A electrician goes to the doctor and tells him he has a hearing problem.

The doctor says, "Please describe the symptoms to me."

The electrician replies, "Homer is a fat yellow lazy man and his wife Marge is skinny with big blue hair."

A guy met his friend walking down the street with a huge bag of burnt out light bulbs.

He asked him what he was going to do with all those useless bulbs.

His friend replied, "I'm going to build a dark room."

An electrician is struggling to find a parking space.

"Lord," he prayed. "I can't stand this. If you open a space up for me, I swear I'll give up the booze and go to church every Sunday."

Suddenly, the clouds part and the sun shines onto an empty parking spot.

Without hesitation, the electrician says, "Never mind Lord, I found one."

I went to my boss at work and said, "I need a raise. Three other companies are after me."

He said, "Really? Which companies are after you?"

I replied, "The electric company, the gas company and the phone company."

An electrician goes into a bar wearing a shirt open at the collar, and is met by a bouncer who tells him that he must wear a necktie to gain admission.

So the electrician goes to his car to try and find a necktie but he can't find one.

However he knows he has some jump leads in his boot; and in desperation he ties these around his neck, and manages to create a knot and lets the ends dangle free.

He goes back to the bar and the bouncer carefully looks him over, and then says, "Well, OK, I guess you can come in - just don't start anything!"

My dopey buddy Peter says he struggles with electricity related puns. He asked me, "Watts so funny about them?"

This electrician called Paddy call up his local paper and asks, "How much would it be to put an ad in your paper?"

"Four pounds an inch," a woman replies. "Why? What are you selling?"

"A ten-foot ladder," said Paddy before slamming the phone down.

A frustrated electrician was sacked by the U.S. Prison Service for refusing to repair an electric chair.

He said that in his opinion, the chair was a #*^*#%* death trap.

A electrician meets up with his blonde girlfriend as she's picking up her car from the repair shop.

"Everything ok with your car now?" he asks.

"Thankfully, yes," the dipsy blonde replies.

He says, "Weren't you worried that the mechanic might try to rip you off?"

She replies, "Yes, but he didn't. I was so relieved when he told me that all I needed was blinker fluid."

His first Christmas, the electrical engineer gave his mother-in-law an electric toothbrush.

The next Christmas, he gave her an electric blanket.

On the third, he gave her an electric carving knife.

Yep, he's working his way up to an electric chair.

A dog walks into a pub, and takes a seat. He says to the barman, "Can I have a pint of lager please."

The barman has never heard a talking dog before and he says, "Wow, that's incredible - you should join the circus."

The dog replies, "Why? Do they need electricians?"

The electrician complained to his friend that his wife didn't satisfy him anymore.

His friend advised he find another woman on the side, pretty sharpish.

When they met up a month or so later, the electrician told his friend, "I took your advice. I managed to find two women on the side, yet my wife still doesn't satisfy me!"

Chapter 5: Longer Electrician Jokes

Three Friends

Ron is chatting to two of his friends, Jim and Shamus.

Jim says, "I think my wife is having an affair with an electrician. The other day I came home and found some wire cutters under our bed and they weren't mine."

Shamus then confides, "Wow, me too! I think my wife is having an affair with a plumber. The other day I found a wrench under the bed and it wasn't mine."

Ron thinks for a minute and then says, "You know something; I think my wife is having an affair with a horse."

Both Jim and Shamus look at him in utter disbelief.

Ron sees them looking at him and says, "No, seriously. The other day I came home early and found a jockey under our bed."

The Electric Chair

A chemist, a biologist and an electrician had all been sentenced to death and were on death row waiting to go to the electric chair.

The chemist goes first. As he strapped him in, the executioner asked him, "Do you have anything you want to say?"

The chemist replied, "No," so the executioner flicked the switch but nothing happened. According to this State's law, if an execution attempt fails, the prisoner has to be released. So the chemist was unstrapped and allowed to walk free.

It was the biologist's turn next. As he was being strapped in, the executioner asked him, "Do you have anything you want to say?"

The biologist replied, "No" so the executioner flicked the switch, but once again nothing happened. So, the biologist was also released.

Then the electrician was brought forward. The executioner asked him, "Do you have anything you want to say?"

The electrician replied, "Yes. If you swap the red and the blue wires over, you might make this thing work."

Three Daughters

A male electrician was talking to two of his friends about their teenage daughters.

The first friend says "I was cleaning my daughter's room the other day and I found a pack of cigarettes. I didn't even know she smoked."

The second friend says, "That's nothing. I was cleaning my daughter's room the other day and I found a half full bottle of Vodka. I didn't even know she drank."

The electrician says, "That's nothing. I was cleaning my daughter's room the other day and I found a pack of condoms. I didn't even know she had a penis."

Exact Words

The homeowner was delighted with the way the electrician had done all the complete re-wiring work on his house.

"You did a great job." he said and handed the man his money. "Also, in order to thank-you, here's an extra 100 dollars to take the missus out to dinner."

Later that night, the doorbell rang and it was the electrician.

The homeowner asked, "What's the matter, did you forget something?"

"Nope." replied the electrician. "I'm just here to take your missus out to dinner like you asked."

The Pearly Gates

An electrician dies in a fishing accident on his 40th birthday and finds himself greeted at the Pearly Gates by a brass band.

Saint Peter runs over, shakes his hand and says "Congratulations!"

"Congratulations for what?" asks the electrician.

"We are celebrating the fact that you lived to be 100 years old." says Saint Peter.

"But that's not true," says the electrician. "I only lived to be forty."

"That's impossible," says Saint Peter, "we added up your time sheets!"

The Clean Floor

A team of electricians were installing a door opening mechanism on my double garage.

I had just finished washing my hall floor when one of the electricians knocked on the back door, and asked to use the toilet.

With dismay I looked at his muddy boots and my newly polished floor.

"Just a minute," I said, "I'll put down some newspaper."

"That's all right, madam," he responded. "I'm house trained."

Twenty Minutes Left To Live

A young electrician is sitting at the bar after work one night, when a big, sweaty construction worker sits down next to him.

They have a few beers together, and start talking about all sorts of subjects, and eventually the conversation gets on to nuclear war.

The electrician asks the construction worker, "If you hear the sirens go off, the missiles are on their way, and you've only got 20 minutes left to live, what would you do?"

The construction worker replies, "That's easy - I'm going to make it with anything that moves."

The construction worker then asks the electrician what he would do to which he replies, "I'm going to try and keep perfectly still."

Three Surgeons

Three surgeons are discussing who makes the best type of surgery patient.

The first surgeon says, "I like to see accountants on my operating table, because when you open them up, everything inside is numbered."

The second surgeon chimes in, "You know, I like working on construction workers. They seem to understand when you have a few parts left over at the end and that the job takes longer than you said it would."

The third responds, "Yeah, but you should try electricians. Everything inside them is colour coded!"

Train Passengers

An electrician, a plumber, a beautiful lady, and an old woman were on a train, sitting 2x2 facing each other.

The train went into a tunnel and the carriage went completely dark, and a loud "thwack" was heard. When the train came out of the tunnel back into the light the plumber had a red hand print on his face. He had been slapped on the face!

The old lady thought, "That plumber must have groped the young lady in the dark and she slapped him."

The hottie thought, "That plumber must have tried to grope me, got the old lady by mistake, and she slapped him."

The plumber thought, "That electrician must have groped the hottie, she thought it was me, and slapped me."

The electrician just sat there thinking, "I can't wait for another tunnel so I can slap that plumber again!"

The Frog

An old electrician was walking through a park when he came across a frog.

He reached down, picked the frog up, and started to put it in his pocket. As he did so, the frog said, "Kiss me on the lips and I'll turn into a beautiful woman and show you a good time."

The old electrician carried on putting the frog in his pocket.

The frog said, "Didn't you hear what I said?"

The electrician looked at the frog and said, "Yes, but at my age I'd rather have a talking frog."

Reunion Lunch

A group of electricians, all aged 40, discussed where they should meet for lunch. They agreed they would meet at a place called The Dog House because the barmaids had big breasts and wore short-skirts.

Ten years later, at age 50, the electricians once again discussed where they should meet for lunch.

It was agreed that they would meet at The Dog House because the food and service was good and there was an excellent beer selection.

Ten years later, at age 60, the friends again discussed where they should meet for lunch.

It was agreed that they would meet at The Dog House because there were plenty of parking spaces, they could dine in peace and quiet, and it was good value for money.

Ten years later, at age 70, the friends discussed where they should meet for lunch.

It was agreed that they would meet at The Dog House because the restaurant was wheelchair accessible and had a toilet for the disabled.

Ten years later, at age 80, the electricians, now all retired, discussed where they should meet for lunch.

Finally it was agreed that they would meet at The Dog House because they had never been there before.

Chapter 6: Electrician Pick-Up Lines

I am an electrician and I know how to turn you on.

You are like a battery, you charge me up.

If you were a burger at McDonald's, you would be the new McShock.

Baby are you the secondary winding to my transformer, I feel magnetically coupled to you.

Want to make a complete circuit together?

You won't believe it but I'm shocking in bed.

Baby your ass is rounder than a motor's rotor.

You are like a 100 Watt halogen bulb, you brighten my world.

You are the light of my life.

You are the perfect switch. You turn me on.

Babe, you sure could light up my night.

I'm an electrician; let me remove your shorts.

I don't usually like being shocked, but when I saw you I was knocked off my feet.

I am an electrician; I want to give you a jolt of my high voltage juice.

Do I turn you on? Because I can.

I'm here to check your shorts.

I'm an electrician and I felt a spark through my body when you entered the room.

Can I earth you? You seem to be at a high potential.

Have you ever met a detective electrician before? Well, hello, they call me Sherlock Ohms.

I'm an electrician; I can turn your lights on.

I know all about power surges.

Chapter 7: Bumper Stickers For Electricians

Electricians do it in the dark.

Get turned on. Sleep with an electrician.

Let an electrician remove your shorts.

Save a fuse. Blow an electrician.

Electricians do it with more frequency and less resistance.

Save a wire. Strip an electrician.

Electricians hang out with strippers all day.

Master electricians do it better.

That's it – I hope you enjoyed the book.

Hey, as a bonus, here are some funny plumber jokes:

Q: Why shouldn't you play poker with a plumber?

A: Because a good flush beats a full house every time.

Q: Why couldn't the plumber get a date?

A: Because he was a real drip.

Q: Why did the plumber keep falling asleep at work?

A: Because his job was draining!

About the author

Chester Croker worked for many years in the building trade and came across many characters, which led to him writing many funny joke books. Chester who is known to his friends as either Chester the Jester or Croker the Joker, was named Comedy Writer Of The Year by the International Jokers Guild.

One final gag: - Did you hear about the cross-eyed electrician? He couldn't see eye to eye with his customers.

I hope you enjoyed this collection of electrician jokes. As you know, some were cheesy, some were corny, and some you may have heard before; but I hope they brought a smile to your face.

If so, kindly leave a review on Amazon so that other electricians can have a good laugh too.

Thanks in advance.

Made in the USA
Monee, IL
29 November 2024

71672083R00038